LOOK AT YOUR BODY
DIGESTION

S<small>TEVE</small> P<small>ARKER</small>

I<small>LLUSTRATED BY</small> I<small>AN</small> T<small>HOMPSON AND</small> S<small>ANDRA</small> D<small>OYLE</small>

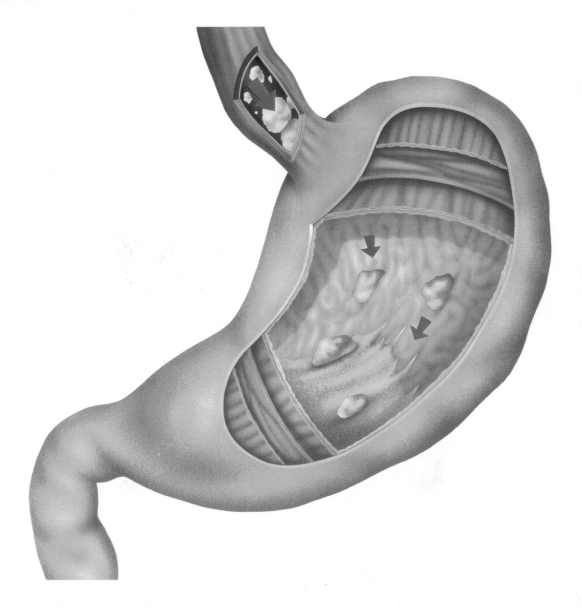

Copper Beech Books
Brookfield, Connecticut

Designed and produced by Aladdin Books Ltd 28 Percy Street London W1P 0LD

First published in the United States in 1997 by Copper Beech Books, an imprint of The Millbrook Press 2 Old New Milford Road Brookfield, Connecticut 06804

Printed in Belgium

Editor Jon Richards

Design David West Children's Book Design *Designer* Rob Perry *Illustrators* Ian Thompson and Sandra Doyle *Picture research* Brooks Krikler Research *Consultant* Dr. R. Levene MB.BS, DCH, DRCOG

Library of Congress Cataloging-in Publication Data
Parker, Steve.
Digestion / Steve Parker: illustrated by Ian Thompson.
p. cm. -- (Look at your body)
Includes index.
ISBN 0-7613-0603-X (lib. bdg.)
1. Digestion--Juvenile literature. 2. Digestive organs--Juvenile literature.
I. Thompson, Ian, 1964-
II. Title. III. Series.
QP145.P164 1997 97-10097
612.3--dc21 CIP

5 4 3 2 1

CONTENTS

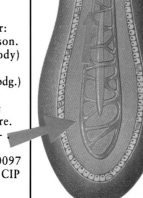

INTRODUCTION

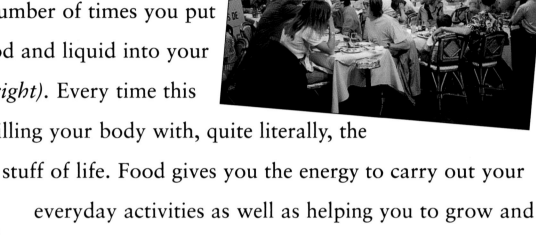

LOOK AT YOUR BODY! Think of the number of times you put food and liquid into your mouth each day *(right)*. Every time this happens you are filling your body with, quite literally, the stuff of life. Food gives you the energy to carry out your everyday activities as well as helping you to grow and maintain your body. Without constant replenishment, your body would wither away and you would starve to death.

However, eating food is only part of the system of events that gets the nutrients into your body. Beyond your mouth is a long "tunnel" down which your food must travel. In this tunnel the food is processed and broken down into microscopic parts that the body can absorb and use.

EATING TO LIVE

LIFE DOES NOT RUN on fresh air alone. Animals and plants need energy to power the thousands of complex chemical processes that occur every second inside their bodies. To do this, living things need to take in nutrients and raw materials, allowing their bodies to grow, develop, maintain themselves, and carry out repairs on any damaged parts.

Your body gets these nutrients and body-building raw materials from the food you eat every day. Different creatures get their food from a wide range of sources. These varying diets can consist of just meat (carnivorous), just plants (herbivorous), or can be a mixture of both plant and animal food (omnivorous).

SUNSHINE DIET
A plant gets its energy from sunlight (above) through the process of photosynthesis. It uses this light to convert raw materials into sugar, which it can burn for energy.

DIRTY DIET
Soil, mud, and earth may not seem very appetizing. But they contain material called humus, which is made up of the decaying bits of animals and plants. Humus is food for earthworms (below), springtails, mites, beetles, slugs, and millions of other soil-living creatures.

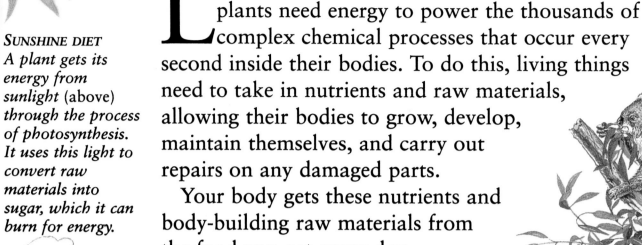

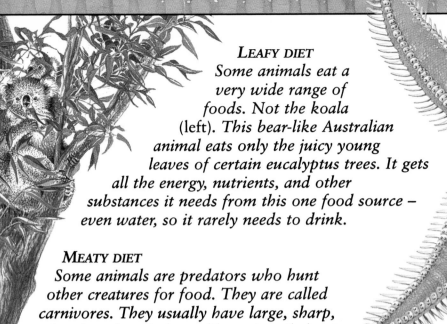

LEAFY DIET
Some animals eat a very wide range of foods. Not the koala (left). *This bear-like Australian animal eats only the juicy young leaves of certain eucalyptus trees. It gets all the energy, nutrients, and other substances it needs from this one food source – even water, so it rarely needs to drink.*

MEATY DIET
Some animals are predators who hunt other creatures for food. They are called carnivores. They usually have large, sharp, pointed teeth and claws, like a tiger (below), to kill and rip up their prey.

EATING OUT
Most animals take food into their bodies, where it is broken down or digested into smaller, simpler components. But the starfish (above) turns its stomach inside out through its mouth and latches onto the flesh of a victim, such as a mussel. Digestive juices dissolve the victim's flesh and the starfish absorbs the soupy results.

INVISIBLE DIET
The water in lakes, rivers, and seas is not perfectly pure. It contains dissolved salts and minerals and tiny floating particles. Some creatures, especially shellfish like barnacles and limpets (right), sieve these nutritious particles from the water as it passes over them. This is called filter-feeding.

PLANT DIET
Plant eaters, or herbivores, like the water buffalo (left), usually have broad, flat teeth for crushing the leaves, shoots, and seeds that they eat. In general, plant food is less nutritious than animal food. So herbivores have to eat more, chewing and digesting it more thoroughly than carnivorous animals.

The NEED FOR FOOD

GROWTH
In only 20 years, the human body grows from a fertilized egg smaller than a pinhead to its full adult size.

ALL THE TIME, your body is using energy. Even asleep, your heart beats, your lungs breathe, and your brain sends and receives nerve signals. All these essential life processes use a level of energy, called your metabolic rate. When you are active and running about, your muscles use even greater quantities of energy, and give off excess heat as a by-product. All this energy comes from your food.

Also, as you grow, you need to make extra body tissues such as bones, muscles, blood, and nerves. The raw materials for these tissues come from food. Even when you are fully grown, the billions of tiny cells inside your body are constantly multiplying, growing, aging, and dying, to be replaced by more cells.

6

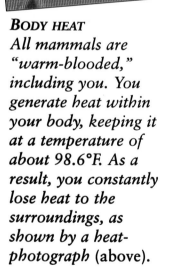

BODY HEAT
All mammals are "warm-blooded," including you. You generate heat within your body, keeping it at a temperature of about 98.6°F. As a result, you constantly lose heat to the surroundings, as shown by a heat-photograph (above).

INJURY AND REPAIR
When the body is ill or injured (right), its cells have to divide faster and work harder to carry out repairs and make replacements. This means the body needs extra supplies of certain nutrients. However, an ill or injured person usually rests too, so he or she needs less energy for movement than if they were fully active.

ENERGY USE

The chart (right) shows the proportion of energy used by each part of the body when resting. The brain is most "energy-hungry." It makes up only one fiftieth of the body's weight, yet it consumes about one fifth of the body's total energy use. The pumping heart also requires plentiful and continuous supplies.

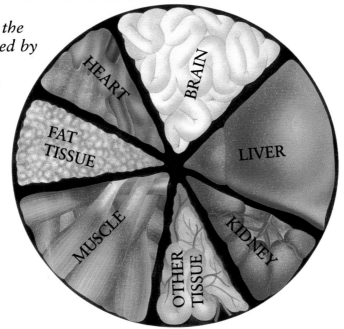

HOW MUCH ENERGY?

Energy and heat are usually measured in units called calories. The more active the body, the more energy it uses (below), both to do the work of moving and in creating the excess heat that makes you feel warm and sweaty.

RUNNING –
7-12 calories per minute. A banana contains enough energy to keep you running for about 5 minutes.

LIFTING –
5-7 calories per minute. A large cabbage leaf contains enough energy for a minute's lifting.

WALKING –
2.4-4.8 calories per minute. The energy from eating a cooked chicken leg powers 30 minutes of walking.

SLEEPING –
0.7-1.2 calories per minute. The energy in a packet of peanuts could keep your basic processes going for 4 hours.

7

A BALANCED DIET

THE FOOD YOU EAT is called your diet. This term is also sometimes used as a short version of "slimming diet" – controlling the food you eat in order to lose weight. The main components of a healthy diet are proteins, carbohydrates, fats, and fiber (see pages 10-11), vitamins and minerals – and of course water, which is essential for all forms of life.

A balanced diet contains a wide range of foods (main picture) and provides a person with enough energy and all the nutrients to keep the body fit and healthy. It should not have too much of one component and should not encourage diet-related diseases (see pages 28-29). Most people also choose foods according to their personal preferences and perhaps religious beliefs.

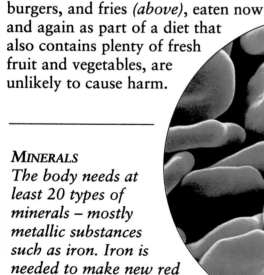

Eating only one or two kinds of food all the time, day after day, can cause health problems. This is true whether the food is carrots, fruit juices, or potato chips. So-called "junk" foods, such as chocolate, candy, cookies, burgers, and fries (above), eaten now and again as part of a diet that also contains plenty of fresh fruit and vegetables, are unlikely to cause harm.

VITAMINS
The body needs small amounts of about 15-20 substances called vitamins. These take part in the various chemical processes within the cells and tissues. Like oil and grease in a car, they ensure the body runs smoothly. Most vitamins come ready-made in a varied, balanced diet. For example, citrus fruits, such as oranges and lemons, are high in Vitamin C, which your body needs for healthy teeth and bones.

MINERALS
The body needs at least 20 types of minerals – mostly metallic substances such as iron. Iron is needed to make new red blood cells (right). But most minerals are needed only in small quantities, and a varied diet contains adequate amounts.

8

WATER

The chemistry of life takes place in a watery medium, with various substances dissolved in water inside the body. About two thirds of your body's weight is made up of water. This is equivalent to some 70 pints of fluid.

Each day your body needs a minimum of around 4.4 pints of water to survive (right). About 1.2 pints comes from foods, 2.6 pints from drinks, and 0.5 pints is metabolic water, made in the body by chemical processes. Your body will get rid of the same amount of water every day. This is lost in urine, feces, sweat, and when you breathe out, ensuring that the levels of water in your body stay balanced.

SUNLIGHT

Vitamin D is produced by your skin naturally when it is exposed to sunlight (below). But be careful! Too much sunlight can be harmful!

METABOLIC WATER

WATER FROM FOOD

WATER FROM DRINK

FOOD FOR THOUGHT

THE MAJOR TYPES of nutrients in a balanced diet are proteins, fats, and carbohydrates – vitamins and minerals are described on the previous pages. Another type of substance, fiber, is also required for health. Each of these major dietary components is needed for a vital role in the body. The job of the digestive system is to take all of these types of foods into the digestive tube or tract and break them down physically and chemically.

Digestive processes split the large food molecules into smaller and smaller units, until finally they are small molecules, tiny enough to pass from the tract into the body itself. The subunits and units can then be reassembled in different combinations to make the cells, tissues, and other parts of the body. In other words – what you eat turns into you.

A diet with too much fat can cause a fatty substance to build up inside arteries *(above)*. These lumps are known as atheroma. If they build up too much, they may block the artery and lead to conditions such as heart disease and high blood pressure. A blockage in one of the arteries supplying blood to the heart may cause a heart attack.

Fats and oils

Animal proteins

Fruit and vegetables

Carbohydrates

THE FOOD PYRAMID
The proportions of foods in a balanced, healthy diet form a "food pyramid" (left). At the base, as a large portion of the total food, are complex carbohydrates found in bread and rice. Plentiful fiber, vitamins, and minerals in fresh vegetables and fruits make up the next layer. Animal proteins are the next layer. Fats and oils are needed in smaller quantities and form the top of the pyramid.

CARBOHYDRATES

The most common forms of carbohydrates are sugars and starches, and they are the body's main energy source. Carbohydrates are found in foods made from cereals, such as bread, and root crops, like potatoes (left).

FATS AND OILS

Certain amounts of fats and oils (right) are required for health. They form the membranes and other parts inside cells, the insulation or sheathing around nerve fibers, and the fatty layer just under the skin that helps to insulate the body and protect it from knocks. Fats also provide some energy.

FIBER

Also called roughage, fiber is not actually digested and taken into the body. But it is needed for health. It gives bulk and substance to food and allows the digestive tract to grip, squeeze, and push along the semi-digested food. Fiber is found mainly in fresh fruits, vegetables, nuts, and similar plant foods (above).

PROTEINS

There are hundreds of different kinds of proteins in the body, and they form the main structural components, parts, and frameworks for cells and tissues. So proteins in the diet are "body-building foods." They are found in meats, fish, dairy produce, and some plant foods, such as nuts (left).

The DIGESTIVE SYSTEM

THE DIGESTIVE SYSTEM takes in food, breaks it down, and absorbs the results into the body. The system is composed of the long digestive tube, running through the body from mouth to anus, plus a few other organs, such as the liver, gall bladder, and pancreas. The whole tract is about 29 ft long. Some sections of the tract, like the stomach, are much wider than others, such as the small intestine. Each section of the tract has its own specialized functions that combine to carry out the overall process of digesting food.

The digestive tract is made of soft tissue and does not show up too well using X rays. If a person takes in the substance called barium, this allows the tract to be seen, since barium shows up in an X ray picture (*above*). It can help identify problems in the digestive tract.

Contraction
of muscles

Movement
of food

MOUTH

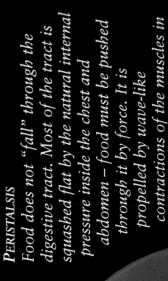

———— FOODPIPE

PERISTALSIS
Food does not "fall" through the digestive tract. Most of the tract is squashed flat by the natural internal pressure inside the chest and abdomen — food must be pushed through it by force. It is propelled by wave-like contractions of the muscles in the tract wall. These waves are called peristalsis (above).

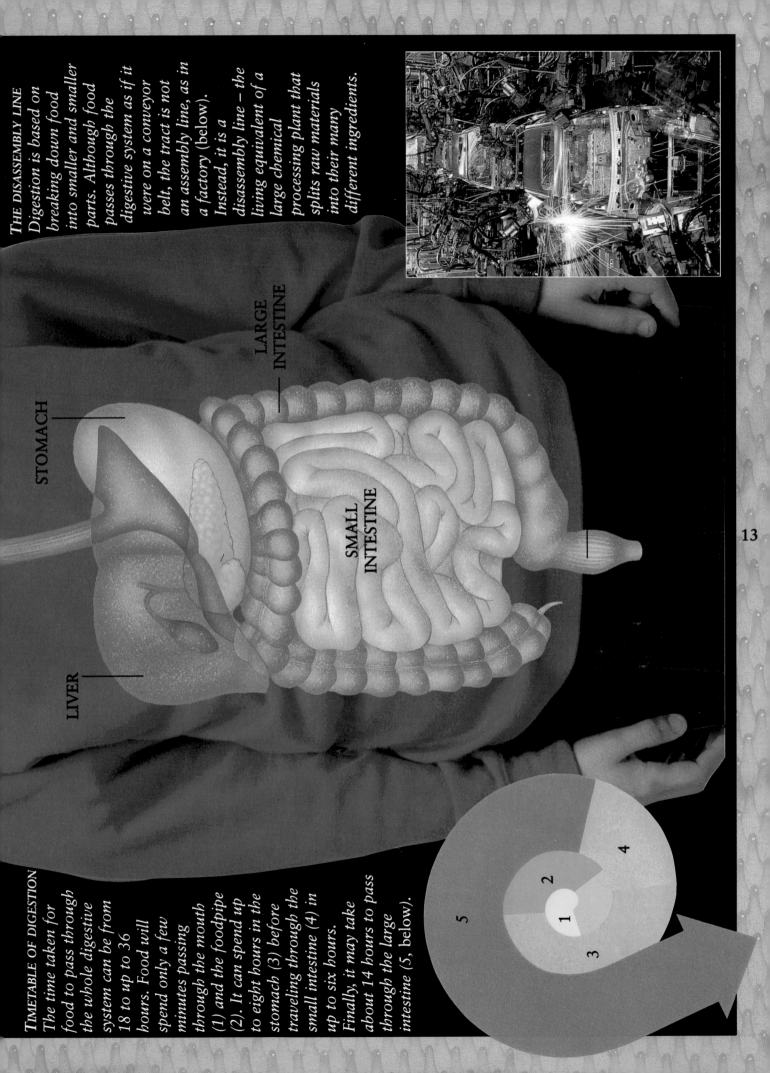

THE DISASSEMBLY LINE
Digestion is based on breaking down food into smaller and smaller parts. Although food passes through the digestive system as if it were on a conveyor belt, the tract is not an assembly line, as in a factory (below). Instead, it is a disassembly line – the living equivalent of a large chemical processing plant that splits raw materials into their many different ingredients.

STOMACH

LARGE INTESTINE

LIVER

SMALL INTESTINE

13

TIMETABLE OF DIGESTION
The time taken for food to pass through the whole digestive system can be from 18 to up to 36 hours. Food will spend only a few minutes passing through the mouth (1) and the foodpipe (2). It can spend up to eight hours in the stomach (3) before traveling through the small intestine (4) in up to six hours. Finally, it may take about 14 hours to pass through the large intestine (5, below).

PAROTID GLAND

TEETH

TONGUE

SUBMANDIBULAR GLAND

SUBLINGUAL GLAND

14

(see page 24)

SALIVARY GLANDS
This cutaway view (left) shows the three pairs of salivary glands, which make a total of about 2.7 pints of saliva each day. A thin tube or duct leads from each gland to empty the saliva into the mouth's interior. The parotid glands are just in front of each ear. The sublingual glands are under each side of the tongue. The submandibular glands are beneath each side of the lower jawbone, called the mandible. Saliva dampens food for easier chewing, makes it slippery for swallowing, and also contains a chemical or enzyme called amylase (see page 24) which begins the breakdown of starchy substances in the food you eat.

SWALLOWING
This is one of the body's most basic automatic or reflex actions. Food is chewed until soft and the tongue pushes up against the hard palate to separate a piece. This is forced back into the throat and into the esophagus (below).

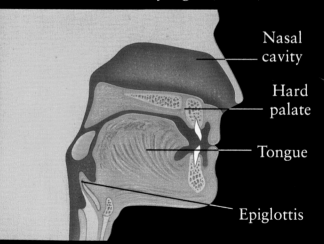

Nasal cavity

Hard palate

Tongue

Epiglottis

BREATHING
The esophagus is squashed flat behind the windpipe. Air flows in through the nose or mouth, down into the top of the windpipe, and into the lungs (right).

SWALLOWING
A stiff flap called the epiglottis tilts over the windpipe automatically to stop swallowed food from going into it (right). If food entered your windpipe, you would choke.

Epiglottis

Nasal cavity

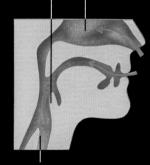

Windpipe

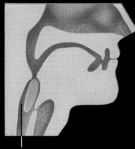

Swallowed food

The MOUTH

THE MOUTH'S MAIN JOBS are to bite small pieces off large items of food, chew these pieces into a soft pulp, and force them down into the foodpipe, or esophagus. Each part of the mouth is adapted to help with these roles. The lips close around food and help to draw it into the mouth's interior *(below)* and stop it from dribbling out. The salivary glands add watery saliva, making dry foods moist and slippery. The tongue tastes food to check that it is not bad or poisonous. It also moves the food around for thorough chewing and pushes it to the back of the mouth where it is swallowed.

A REAL MOUTHFUL
Humans and most other mammals have strong teeth at the front of the mouth to bite pieces off food. But some animals have to swallow their prey whole. Most snakes can make their jaw open extremely wide – they can swallow something bigger than their head! The egg-eating snake (above) swallows whole eggs, crushing their shells to release the contents.

THE UVULA
At the back of your mouth hangs a fleshy cone, the uvula (above). This stops food from entering the nasal cavity when swallowing.

15

SUCKING
Muscle movements of the mouth and chest can expand the air space in the mouth, windpipe, and lungs, creating low pressure inside the mouth. This allows us to suck up liquids or sloppy foods such as soup. As the air pressure inside the mouth reduces, normal atmospheric pressure outside the mouth pushes the drink up into the mouth.

The TEETH

THE SIZE, SHAPE, AND NUMBER of an animal's teeth are a good indication of the type of food it eats. Over millions of years, specialized hunters like cats and dogs have evolved long, sharp teeth, while herbivores such as cows and deer have developed broad, flat ones.

The shape of human teeth indicates that we have evolved as omnivores, able to eat both plant and animal food. Your teeth consist of sharp incisors and canine teeth at the front, as well as flat, broad molars at the back. With care these teeth should last you a lifetime.

HUNTING TEETH
The shark has the typical teeth of a hunter (left) – *blade-shaped and sharp-edged for sawing through flesh and gristle.*

ORAL HYGIENE
Brushing teeth (right) *gets rid of old food and the microbes that feed on it. Toothpaste* (above) *helps this and often provides the mineral fluoride for stronger teeth. Floss removes fragments of food stuck between teeth. Mouthwash* (left) *keeps the whole mouth clean and free of bad breath smells.*

GUM

CEMENT

THE DENTIST
Most people are advised to visit the dentist at least once each year (right). *The dentist can check for signs of decay and other problems, and treat these at an early stage. The hygienist gives advice on keeping teeth clean.*

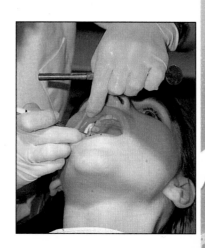

16

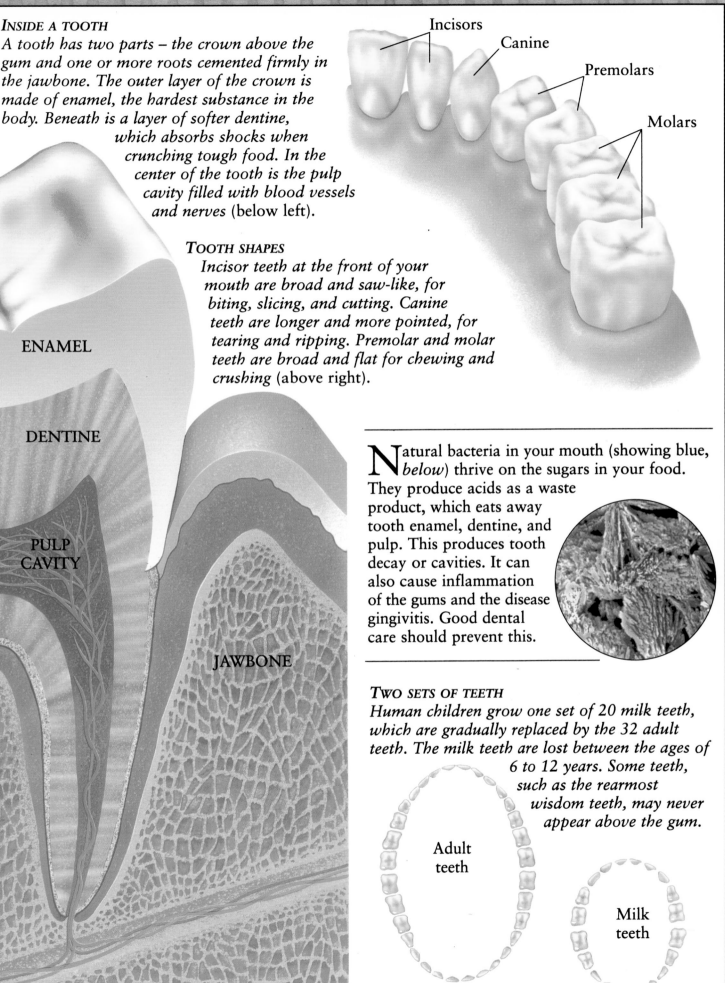

INSIDE A TOOTH

A tooth has two parts – the crown above the gum and one or more roots cemented firmly in the jawbone. The outer layer of the crown is made of enamel, the hardest substance in the body. Beneath is a layer of softer dentine, which absorbs shocks when crunching tough food. In the center of the tooth is the pulp cavity filled with blood vessels and nerves (below left).

Incisors

Canine

Premolars

Molars

TOOTH SHAPES

Incisor teeth at the front of your mouth are broad and saw-like, for biting, slicing, and cutting. Canine teeth are longer and more pointed, for tearing and ripping. Premolar and molar teeth are broad and flat for chewing and crushing (above right).

ENAMEL

DENTINE

PULP CAVITY

JAWBONE

Natural bacteria in your mouth (showing blue, *below*) thrive on the sugars in your food. They produce acids as a waste product, which eats away tooth enamel, dentine, and pulp. This produces tooth decay or cavities. It can also cause inflammation of the gums and the disease gingivitis. Good dental care should prevent this.

TWO SETS OF TEETH

Human children grow one set of 20 milk teeth, which are gradually replaced by the 32 adult teeth. The milk teeth are lost between the ages of 6 to 12 years. Some teeth, such as the rearmost wisdom teeth, may never appear above the gum.

Adult teeth

Milk teeth

INTO THE STOMACH

THE STOMACH IS A MUSCULAR-WALLED, J-shaped bag found in the upper-left abdomen *(right)*. It has three main roles in digestion. It stores the food from a large meal, expanding to hold up to 3.5 pints of swallowed food. It also squirms and squeezes these contents by contractions of the three muscle layers in its walls to continue the physical breakdown of food begun by chewing in the mouth.

Finally, the stomach also makes various gastric juices in its lining, adding these to the food to cause chemical breakdown and digestion (see pages 24-25). Stomach acid also helps to kill any microbes that may have been swallowed in contaminated food.

18

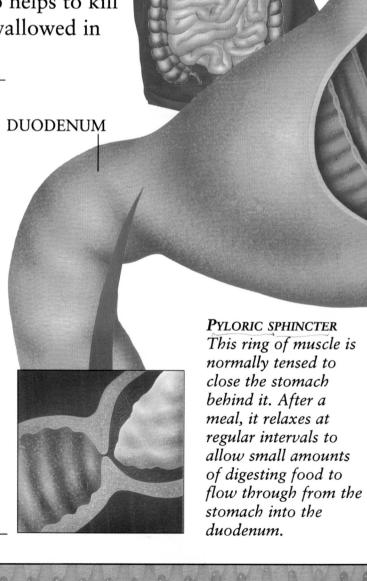

DUODENUM

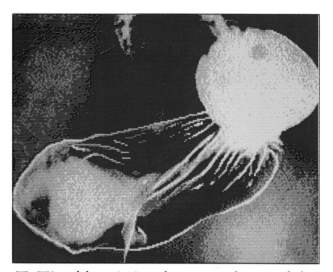

Hiatal hernia involves a weakness of the diaphragm, the sheet of muscle above the stomach and liver that separates the chest from the abdomen. The weakness allows part of the upper stomach to stick through the diaphragm into the chest (see X ray, *above*). Acidic stomach contents may then well up into the lower esophagus. This is called acid reflux. It causes a pain, commonly known as heartburn.

PYLORIC SPHINCTER
This ring of muscle is normally tensed to close the stomach behind it. After a meal, it relaxes at regular intervals to allow small amounts of digesting food to flow through from the stomach into the duodenum.

LONGITUDINAL
MUSCLE LAYER

CIRCULAR
MUSCLE LAYER

OBLIQUE
MUSCLE LAYER

STOMACH
LINING

SWALLOWED
FOOD

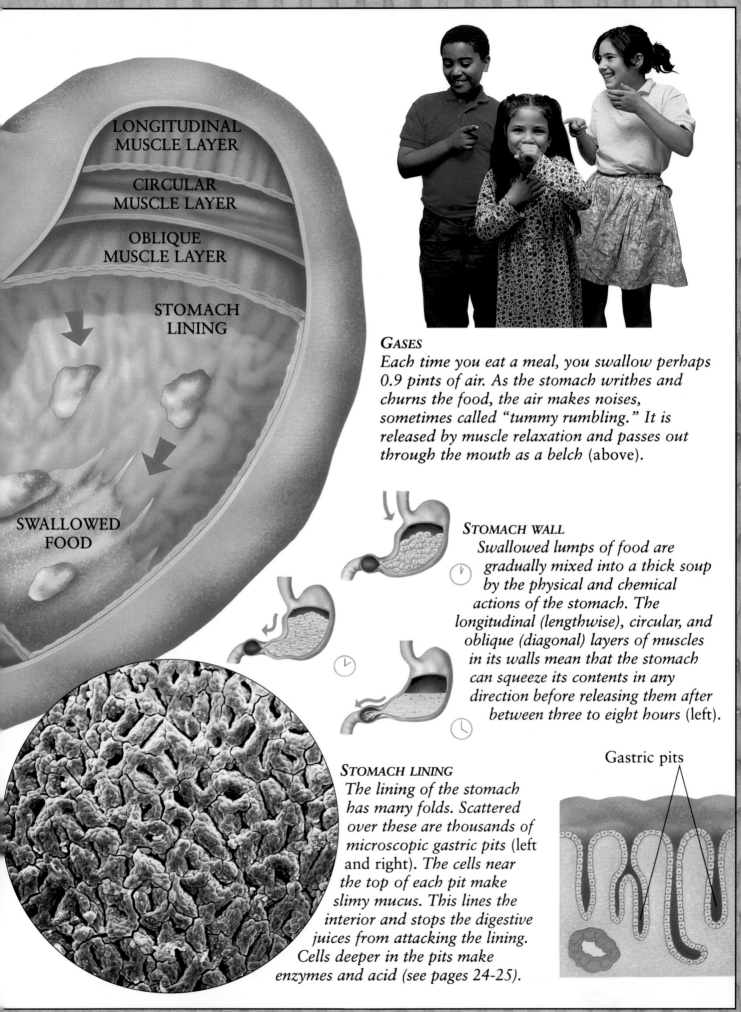

GASES

Each time you eat a meal, you swallow perhaps 0.9 pints of air. As the stomach writhes and churns the food, the air makes noises, sometimes called "tummy rumbling." It is released by muscle relaxation and passes out through the mouth as a belch (above).

STOMACH WALL

Swallowed lumps of food are gradually mixed into a thick soup by the physical and chemical actions of the stomach. The longitudinal (lengthwise), circular, and oblique (diagonal) layers of muscles in its walls mean that the stomach can squeeze its contents in any direction before releasing them after between three to eight hours (left).

Gastric pits

STOMACH LINING

The lining of the stomach has many folds. Scattered over these are thousands of microscopic gastric pits (left and right). The cells near the top of each pit make slimy mucus. This lines the interior and stops the digestive juices from attacking the lining. Cells deeper in the pits make enzymes and acid (see pages 24-25).

The SMALL INTESTINE

The "SMALL" INTESTINE *(right)* is the longest part of the digestive tract, at almost 19 ft. (6 m). However, it is also the narrowest, only 1.5 in. (4 cm) in diameter. It has three sections. First is the duodenum, which receives food from the stomach. It is about 10 in. (25 cm) long, and the section where most of the final stages of chemical digestion occur.

Second is the jejunum, about 8ft. (2.5 m) long, where some of the products of digestion are absorbed through the lining, into tiny blood vessels.

Third is the ileum, about 10ft. (3 m) long, where the final stages of digestion occur. The digesting food may take six hours to trickle along the small intestine before reaching the next part of the tract, the large intestine (see pages 26-27).

STRAIGHTENED OUT
The small intestine is coiled to fill most of the abdomen. If it were straight, the human body would be almost 22 ft. (7 m) tall, and very thin!

20

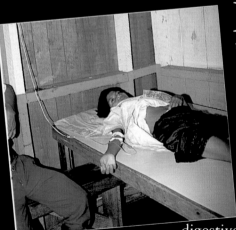

Digestive infections, such as those caused by the typhoid and cholera bacteria *(right)*, can make the tract swollen and inflamed. The sufferer passes great quantities of very dilute, runny diarrhea. This contains vital water, salts, and minerals, especially sodium, potassium, and chloride, that would normally be absorbed by the digestive tract. If the situation is caught soon enough, a balanced watery solution of salts and minerals, to replenish the body's supplies, can be given through the mouth. This is called ORT – oral rehydration therapy. If the patient becomes seriously infected, emergency treatment, in the form of a drip *(above)*, may be required.

INTESTINE LINING
The small intestine is
not a plain tube. Its
lining has many
folds and projections
called villi (right).
These provide a
huge surface area for
absorbing food.

Lymph tube ——————

Capillaries ——————

Villus cells ——————

INSIDE A VILLUS
Each villus (right) houses
a network of microscopic
blood capillaries and a
tiny lymph tube.
Digested nutrients are
small enough to
pass through the
cells covering the
villus, into the blood and
lymph to be carried away.

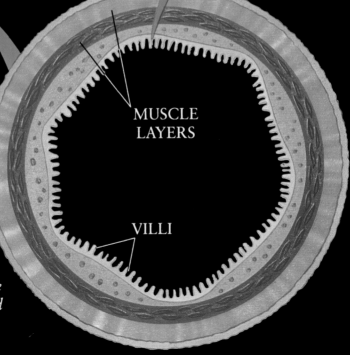

MUSCLE
LAYERS

VILLI

LAYERS OF INTESTINE
This cross-section through the small
intestine (right) shows the villi
and folds of the lining and the
two layers of muscles in the
wall. The muscles
continue the process of
moving the food along
as they force the runny,
digested food along the
digestive tract, toward
the large intestine.

LIVER, GALL BLADDER, & PANCREAS

THESE ORGANS are not part of the digestive tract, but they are part of the digestive system. The liver is the body's largest gland, deep red and rich in blood. It fills the upper-right part of the abdomen *(right)*. It is like a living chemical factory and nutrient-processing center, with at least 500 different roles in your body's chemical reactions. Here, nutrients from digested food are broken down, processed, and stored. The pancreas makes strong digestive juices, which are added to the digesting food. The gall bladder stores bile, a by-product from the liver that also helps with digestion.

In some people, hard lumps called gall stones form in the gall bladder (showing blue, *left*). If they try to leave the gall bladder along the cystic and bile ducts, they cause an intense pain known as biliary colic. Treatments include drugs to dissolve the stones, surgery to remove them, and high-energy ultrasound to shatter them into tiny pieces.

THE GALL BLADDER
This is a storage bag for bile, a greenish yellow liquid made by the liver as it breaks down and recycles red blood cells. When food passes into the small intestine, the gall bladder expels its bile along a duct. The bile is joined by more bile flowing directly from the liver. This then flows along the common bile duct and empties into the duodenum, where it helps to break down large fat molecules.

Duct leading from liver

Duct

Gall bladder

Common bile duct

Duodenum

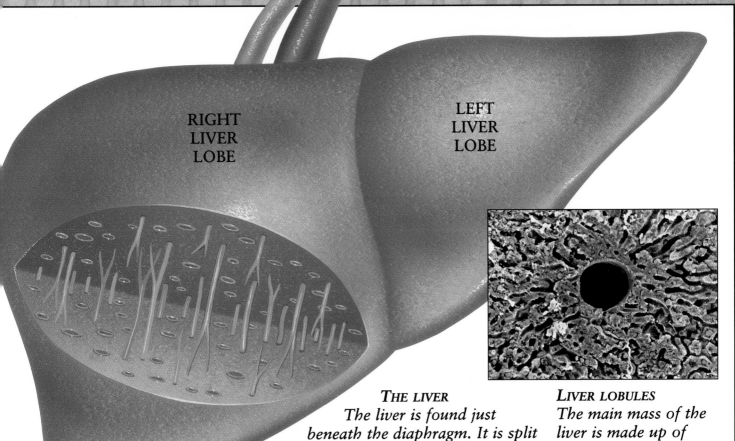

RIGHT
LIVER
LOBE

LEFT
LIVER
LOBE

THE LIVER
The liver is found just beneath the diaphragm. It is split into two parts, or lobes (above), which are divided by a ligament. The right lobe is slightly larger and has the gall bladder tucked under it, while the left lobe extends over the stomach. About one third of the blood the liver receives is rich in oxygen. It uses this oxygen to power its many roles. The rest of the blood the liver receives is loaded with nutrients from the small intestine. One of the liver's roles is to store carbohydrates for times when your body's energy supplies run low.

LIVER LOBULES
The main mass of the liver is made up of thousands of tiny units called hepatic lobules (above). Each has cells called hepatocytes, which carry out the liver's chemical roles. Running through each lobule are a tiny artery and vein for blood, a bile tube, and a lymph tube.

THE PANCREAS
The pancreas is a soft, tapering gland with two tubes or ducts leading from it (below right). Its digestive function is to make powerful enzymes and other digestive juices in the acinar cells (right above), which make up most of its mass. These juices flow along the two ducts into the duodenum. The pancreas' other role is to make hormones, including insulin.

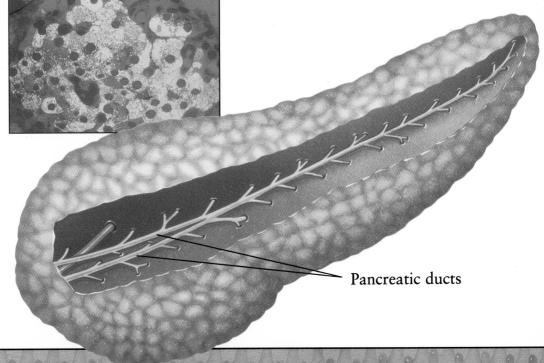

Pancreatic ducts

The CHEMICAL SOUP

A T LEAST FIFTY DIGESTIVE CHEMICALS selectively attack the proteins, carbohydrates, fats, and the other components of food, breaking them down into smaller parts. These chemicals are mostly enzymes – substances that alter the rate at which chemical changes take place. Human digestive enzymes speed up the chopping of food molecules into smaller and smaller parts, while the food progresses farther along the digestive tract.

Many enzymes made by the lining of the digestive tract are inactive when they are produced. They will only start to work under certain conditions, such as the right levels of acidity. This system prevents the enzymes from digesting the cells that produced them!

CONTROL OF DIGESTION

The activities of the digestive processes are coordinated by nerves and hormones. As food is swallowed, the stomach is stimulated to release the hormone gastrin. This causes cells in the stomach lining to release stomach acids. It also affects the nerves controlling the squeezing motion of the stomach (see page 19).

UNDER LOCK AND KEY

Digestive enzymes work on the "lock-and-key" principle. In the "soup" of digesting food, enzymes (green, left) mix with food particles (pink).

Just as certain keys will only open certain locks, so certain enzymes work on certain food particles. Once the enzyme has found the correct food particle, they bind together, and the food particle breaks down for absorption (right).

1 MOUTH

As you eat your food, the salivary glands in your mouth release saliva (see page 14). Contained within saliva is an enzyme called salivary amylase. During chewing, this enzyme helps break up huge starch molecules found in carbohydrate-rich foods. These molecules are broken down into simpler sugars, such as maltose and dextrin, which are broken down again farther along the digestive tract (see below). The rest of the saliva helps form the food into small "parcels" and lubricates these while you swallow them.

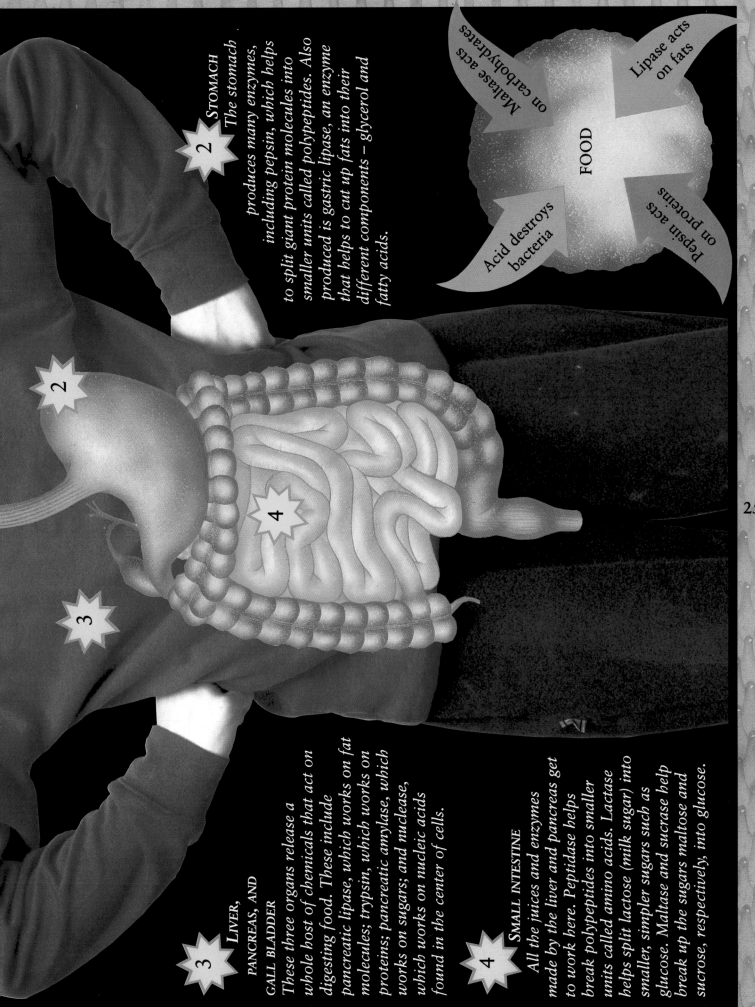

FOOD

Maltase acts on carbohydrates

Lipase acts on fats

Acid destroys bacteria

Pepsin acts on proteins

2 STOMACH
The stomach produces many enzymes, including pepsin, which helps to split giant protein molecules into smaller units called polypeptides. Also produced is gastric lipase, an enzyme that helps to cut up fats into their different components – glycerol and fatty acids.

3 LIVER, PANCREAS, AND GALL BLADDER
These three organs release a whole host of chemicals that act on digesting food. These include pancreatic lipase, which works on fat molecules; trypsin, which works on proteins; pancreatic amylase, which works on sugars; and nuclease, which works on nucleic acids found in the center of cells.

4 SMALL INTESTINE
All the juices and enzymes made by the liver and pancreas get to work here. Peptidase helps break polypeptides into smaller units called amino acids. Lactase helps split lactose (milk sugar) into smaller, simpler sugars such as glucose. Maltase and sucrase help break up the sugars maltose and sucrose, respectively, into glucose.

The LARGE INTESTINE

THE LARGE INTESTINE is not the widest part of the digestive tract, nor the longest. But it is the bulkiest. It measures some 3.5 ft. long and has five main sections. First is the cecum, a pouch-like chamber at the end of the small intestine. Branching from this is the second section, the small, finger-sized dead-end tube of the appendix. Next is the colon, which forms a "frame" around the small intestine. This leads to the fourth section, the rectum, and finally the end of the entire digestive tract, the anus.

The lining of the large intestine only produces mucus and absorbs water and a few minerals from the digested food.

The finger-shaped appendix seems to have no obvious role in the digestive process. In babies and children, it may be involved in helping the body to develop protection or immunity against certain diseases. The appendix normally comes to notice only if it gets blocked with digestive matter and bacteria. Should this happen, it becomes inflamed and extremely painful. This condition is called appendicitis. The appendix may then be removed by the operation called an appendectomy *(left)*.

MUCUS SECRETIONS
The only substance secreted by the large intestine is mucus. This is released by tiny goblet cells in the intestine lining (below). The mucus protects the intestine wall and helps lubricate the waste matter as it passes through the rest of the large intestine.

Large intestine absorbs a lot of water and some minerals

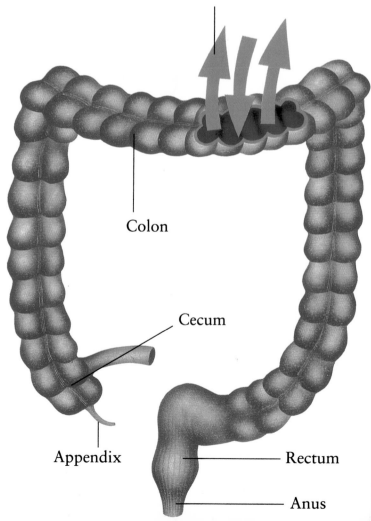

Colon

Cecum

Appendix

Rectum

Anus

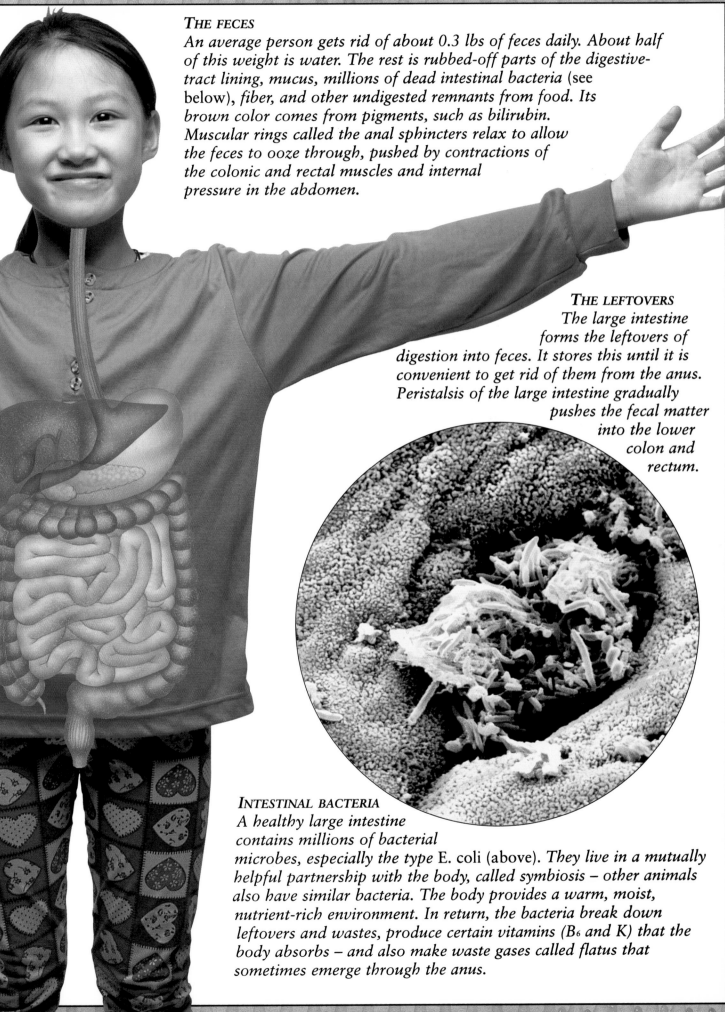

THE FECES

An average person gets rid of about 0.3 lbs of feces daily. About half of this weight is water. The rest is rubbed-off parts of the digestive-tract lining, mucus, millions of dead intestinal bacteria (see below), fiber, and other undigested remnants from food. Its brown color comes from pigments, such as bilirubin. Muscular rings called the anal sphincters relax to allow the feces to ooze through, pushed by contractions of the colonic and rectal muscles and internal pressure in the abdomen.

THE LEFTOVERS

The large intestine forms the leftovers of digestion into feces. It stores this until it is convenient to get rid of them from the anus. Peristalsis of the large intestine gradually pushes the fecal matter into the lower colon and rectum.

INTESTINAL BACTERIA

A healthy large intestine contains millions of bacterial microbes, especially the type E. coli (above). They live in a mutually helpful partnership with the body, called symbiosis – other animals also have similar bacteria. The body provides a warm, moist, nutrient-rich environment. In return, the bacteria break down leftovers and wastes, produce certain vitamins (B_6 and K) that the body absorbs – and also make waste gases called flatus that sometimes emerge through the anus.

DIETARY PROBLEMS

THE DIGESTIVE SYSTEM can be affected by various kinds of problems and hazards. In the modern world, the main one is malnourishment, which causes misery, hunger, disease, and starvation for millions of people.

The digestive tract is also prone to infection from bacteria and viruses, including salmonella, listeria, dysentery, and cholera, which are also responsible for causing a great many illnesses and deaths. Some of these are spread by drinking contaminated water.

There are also digestive infestations of internal pests and parasites, such as tapeworms, roundworms, threadworms, and flukes. Other problems include food allergies and consuming poisonous foods, such as certain mushrooms.

EATING AND BEHAVIOR
Some psychological or behavioral problems affect eating habits. In anorexia, a person feels that he or she is overweight and eats less and less, becoming very thin (above). Some people show compulsive eating behavior and become obese. A food phobia is a fear of certain foods.

28

DIGESTIVE PARASITES
For a parasite, the digestive tract is a wonderful place – warm, wet, and full of nutritious substances. The result is that the parasite "steals" food from its host. The tapeworm (left and above) anchors itself into the intestine using tiny hooks and suckers on its head. It has no mouth, but absorbs nutrients through its thin skin. It gets these nutrients by "stealing" them from food that the host has eaten.

DEFICIENCY DISEASES

Lack of nutritious food, especially vitamins and minerals (see pages 8-9), may cause deficiency diseases. For example, lack of vitamin D causes a weakness of the bones, known as rickets in children and osteomalacia in adults. In this disease the bones in the legs may bend under the body's weight (right). Vitamin D is normally found in fish, butter, and eggs, or it can be made in the skin when exposed to sunlight (see page 9).

Just as other parts of the body may react to certain normally harmless substances, so the digestive tract may be allergic or extra-sensitive to certain foods. Common examples of these foods are eggs, shellfish, and cheese. Coeliac disease is due to an abnormal sensitivity to gluten, a protein in wheat, rye, and similar grains. It makes the lining of the small intestine swollen and inflamed. However, in some suspected food allergies, the symptoms may be vague and generalized and the culprit food is difficult to track down.

29

EATING JUST ENOUGH

In the wealthy, industrialized parts of the world, probably the most common diet-related problem is obesity – being overweight. Eating too much means the body converts the excess sugars into fat, or adipose tissue, and lays it down for storage. Obesity brings increased risks of many health problems, from heart disease to high blood pressure.

POISONS

As well as natural poisons, powerful chemicals such as bleaches, solvents, and paints (below) can cause great problems or even death if they are swallowed. All dangerous chemicals and substances should be kept safe.

KNOW YOUR BODY!

YOUR TEETH ARE COVERED *in a very tough substance called enamel – it's the toughest stuff in your body. This helps them to withstand enormous pressures encountered as you grind and chew the food you eat. Toughest of all your teeth are the molars at the back of your mouth (left). They are able to take pressures of up to 170 lbs./sq. in.*

THE FINGER-LIKE VILLI (right) *that line most of your digestive system play a vital role in absorbing nutrients from your food. They greatly increase the area across which these nutrients can be absorbed. Without them your digestive system would have to be 2.25 miles long to have the same area.*

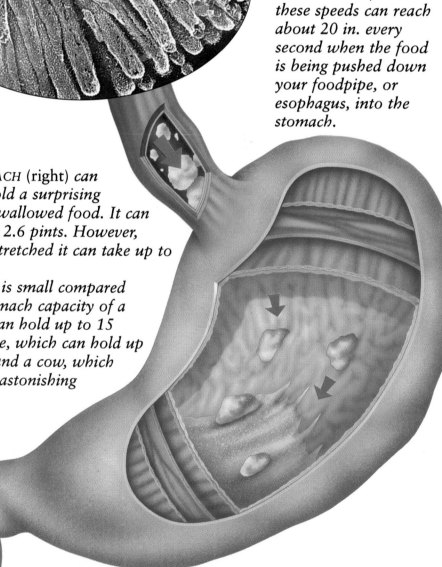

WAVES OF PERISTALSIS (above) *can move food around your digestive system at an amazing rate. At their fastest, these speeds can reach about 20 in. every second when the food is being pushed down your foodpipe, or esophagus, into the stomach.*

YOUR STOMACH (right) *can stretch to hold a surprising amount of swallowed food. It can usually hold 2.6 pints. However, when fully stretched it can take up to 7 pints!*

    Even this is small compared with the stomach capacity of a pig, which can hold up to 15 pints, a horse, which can hold up to 35 pints and a cow, which can hold an astonishing 264 pints.

EVERY DAY, *your body makes 12 pints of digestive fluids. This includes 2.6 pints of saliva, 1.7 pints of bile, 2.6 pints of pancreatic juice, and 5.1 pints of intestinal juices.*

GLOSSARY

Acinar cells – The tiny cells found in the pancreas that produce the powerful digestive juices released into the small intestine.

Atheroma – The lumps of fatty plaque that build up inside arteries if a diet contains too much fat.

Bile – The greenish-yellow fluid produced by the liver when it breaks down red blood cells. It is useful in digestion, where it breaks down fats.

Calorie – The unit for measuring energy.

Carbohydrates – Made from carbon, oxygen, and hydrogen, these parts of your food are used by your body to give you energy.

Carnivores – Meat-eating animals such as lions, tigers, or sharks.

Digestion – The breakdown, both physically and chemically, of food, and the absorption of the important parts into your body.

Enzymes – These are chemicals that increase the rate of a chemical change or reaction. In the case of digestion they break down large food particles to help the body absorb them.

Epiglottis – The small flap at the back of your throat that closes over the windpipe to prevent you from choking while swallowing food.

Fats – These parts of your food are used by the body to build membranes. They also supply a small amount of energy.

Fiber – The body does not digest this part of your food. However, it is needed to help push food through the digestive tract.

Herbivores – Plant-eating animals such as cows, deer, and sheep.

Liver lobules – The tiny units that make up most of the liver. They carry out the liver's chemical roles.

Minerals – These substances in your food are used by the body to make new parts, such as red blood cells, which need the mineral iron.

Mucus – The thick, sticky substance produced by the body to protect certain parts and lubricate the movement of food through the digestive tract.

Omnivores – Animals that can eat all types of food, both plant and meat. These include pigs and humans.

Parasites – Foreign organisms that live on or inside another body, taking nutrients.

Peristalsis – The wave-like contractions of the muscles in your digestive tract that push food along it.

Photosynthesis – The conversion by plants of carbon dioxide and water into sugars using sunlight. A waste product of this is oxygen.

Proteins – The parts of your food that your body breaks down and uses to build structural components, such as the walls of your body's cells.

Sphincter – A circular muscle that helps keep an opening or tube closed.

Villi – The tiny finger-like projections that stick out from the intestine lining. These aid absorption by providing a greater area than a smooth surface.

Vitamins – These important substances are vital for health and to help your body run smoothly.

INDEX

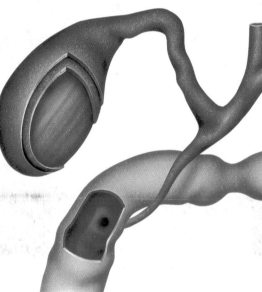

Photo credits:
Abbreviations: t-top, m-middle, b-bottom, r-right, l-left

Cover m, 5, 6m, 8b, 10, 12b, 17m, 18m, 19b, 20m, 20-21, 21t, 22m, 23 both, 26 both, 27, 28m, 29t & 30m – Science Photo Library. Cover b, 3b, 6-7, 7 all, 8m, 8-9, 10-11, 11 all, 12-13, 14, 15 all, 16m, 18t, 19t, 20t, 22t, 24-25, 26-27, 28-29, 29m&b, & 32 all – Roger Vlitos. 3t & 6m – Rex Features. 13t – Rover Cars. 16b & 28t – Frank Spooner Pictures.